A RITUAL FOR
HOLOCAUST REMEMBRANCE

LIGHT
FROM THE
DARKNESS

Deborah Fripp and Violet Neff-Helms

BEHRMAN HOUSE

www.behrmanhouse.com

This is for the murdered millions, and dedicated to the great-grandchildren, our enduring triumph.

The authors and publisher gratefully acknowledge these editorial consultants for their contributions:

- Rabbi Geoffrey Dennis, Congregation Kol Ami, Flower Mound, Texas
- Dr. Michael Fripp, educator, Congregation Kol Ami, Flower Mound, Texas
- Ellen Rank, The Jewish Education Project, New York
- Rabbi Perry Rank, Midway Jewish Center, Syosset, New York
- Rabbi Jonah Rank, Kehilat HaNahar, New Hope, Pennsylvania
- Lynne Ravas, Holocaust educator, Echoes and Reflections, Carnegie, Pennsylvania
- Rabbi Danny Zemel, Temple Micah, Washington, DC
- Diane Zimmerman, associate educator, Temple Sinai, Washington, DC

Behrman House, Inc.
Millburn, New Jersey 07041
www.behrmanhouse.com

ISBN 978-1-68115-011-6

Library of Congress Cataloging-in-Publication Data
Names: Fripp, Deborah, 1970- author. | Neff-Helms, Violet, author.
Title: Light from the darkness : a ritual for Holocaust remembrance /
    Deborah Fripp and Violet Neff-Helms.
Description: Millburn : Behrman House, [2020] | "This ritual of remembrance is loosely based on the Passover
    seder, with familiar elements adapted to the modern context: drinking cups of wine, dipping in salt water,
    spilling drops of wine, asking questions"--Introduction. | Summary: "Filled with song and story, ritual and
    remembrance, this short and empowering guided experience helps us do what Holocaust survivors have
    always asked of us: to tell the story, to remember, and to act"-- Provided by publisher.
Identifiers: LCCN 2019034520 | ISBN 9781681150116 (paperback)
Subjects: LCSH: Holocaust, Jewish (1939–1945)--Religious aspects. |
    Holocaust, Jewish (1939–1945)--Anniversaries, etc. |
    Haggadah--Adaptations.
Classification: LCC D804.7.R45 F75 2020 | DDC 296.4--dc23
LC record available at https://lccn.loc.gov/2019034520

Printed in the United States of America
9 8 7 6 5 4 3 2 1

Edited by Aviva Lucas Gutnick
Cover design by Cassie Gonzales
Book design by Zatar Creative

CONTENTS

SYMBOLS

HERE ARE THE SYMBOLS WE WILL ENCOUNTER AND USE IN THIS EXPERIENCE: (Find preparation tips on page 38.)

Mismatched candlesticks: in recognition of the resilience of our ancestors

A child's drawing: representing our hopes for our children

Rosemary sprigs: for the sweet, flavorful life we had

Unpeeled oranges: for hope that can live beneath bitterness

Wine: in celebration of life

Fruit with pits: for inner strength and an unbreakable core

Potato skins dipped in salt water: for the tears we shed in times of starvation

Yahrtzeit **candle:** in memory of the murdered millions

Sweet tea: for Kiddush when we could not get wine

Bread/Challah: in celebration of community

INTRODUCTION

Today we journey through one of the darkest chapters in our history. Yet we recognize that darkness is tempered by light. As has happened so often in our history, powerful people tried to destroy us, body and soul, but they failed. Many were murdered, more than we can ever truly comprehend, an incalculable loss. But the Jewish people survived, strengthened in our resolve to remain Jews.

Today we celebrate our survival and our strength, even as we honor our lost and remember the horrific hatred and violence that we endured.

Emerging from that horror, we felt broken. We began to collect the slivers of that battered life. Today we will use the sacred remnants of the past to create a new ritual, steeped in tradition. This ritual of remembrance is loosely based on the Passover seder, with familiar elements adapted to the modern context: drinking cups of wine, dipping in salt water, spilling drops of wine, asking questions.

Why use the seder as a model? At the seder, we tell the story of our survival from a great tragedy—four hundred years of slavery. We mourn the bitterness of the Egyptian slavery while celebrating our passage to freedom. Today, we will tell the story of our survival from another great tragedy. We will mourn the losses of the Holocaust while celebrating our survival as a people.

Today, we remember real people. We will hear their voices. We will speak their names. We will take inspiration from their resilience and the strength of those who stood up for each other in the most difficult circumstances.

LIGHT FROM DARKNESS

We have been broken. Part of us will always be broken. We gather each precious shard and piece them together to create a new vessel that will hold our love and our pain.

We find that we are somehow whole and broken at the same time. We discover glimmers of holiness in the cracks, for it is through these jagged windows that we see the paths to building a better world.

There is more to a broken vessel than the hammer that shattered it.

READ TOGETHER:

> Even when we are enveloped by evil, we hold on to our humanity and our faith. We emerge as a Jewish people strengthened in our resolve to remain Jews. The thread of Jewish life was—and still is—strong.

"Blessed is the match consumed in kindling flame. Blessed is the flame that burns in the secret fastness of the heart."
(**Hannah Senesh,** Holocaust refugee, left safety of Palestine to fight in Hungary)

Rose and Barbed Wire,
Shmuel Leitner

אוֹר מֵחֹשֶׁךְ

CANDLE LIGHTING

These mismatched candlesticks remind us of the resilience that our ancestors have always shown in dark times. They made do with what they had. They never gave up their determination to hold on to their Judaism.

We take inspiration from their resilience and from those who found the strength to stand when standing seemed impossible.

LIGHT THE CANDLES AND RECITE:

We light these candles for the light that shines in the hearts of all who fight against evil, for "a single candle can both defy and define the darkness" (**Anonymous**).

Often Jews had to sell their silver candlesticks to survive in the ghetto. Nonetheless, many people continued to light candles, even if they no longer had fancy candlesticks.

ORIGINS · מְקוֹרוֹת

We begin our story in the light.

We remember:

Not so long ago, many of our mothers and our fathers, our sisters and our brothers, lived in the land of Europe.

We were Jews of many different sorts. We were religious and secular. We lived in cities and in small towns. We lived in many countries across the world. We spoke many different languages. We were doctors and dressmakers, printers and poets, scientists and shopkeepers, weavers and welders.

"We were a warm family whose life followed a quiet, carefree routine. Our roots reached back generation upon generation, living there amidst friends, neighbors, and acquaintances. With this loving background, the years flowed peacefully." (**Miriam Yahav**, Holocaust survivor, Poland)

An ancient hatred, unashamed, was emerging from the shadows, but we did not recognize the approaching danger. We thought the world was evolving beyond such ignorance.

"My Polish neighbors were my best friends. I loved to play hide-and-seek with them in the garden behind our house. In the winter, when the water froze, we loved to run and slide on the slippery ice; and in the spring, when the ice melted, we made paper boats and launched them on the water, chasing them along the bank until they disappeared from view." (**Hannah Gofrit**, Holocaust survivor, Poland)

OUR SWEET, FLAVORFUL LIFE

The fragrant rosemary recalls for us the joys of an ordinary life.

View of Ostende with Boat, 1935, Felix Nussbaum, gouache on paper

SMELL THE ROSEMARY AND RECITE:

We remember the sweet, flavorful life we had before the darkness fell.

Blessed are You, Adonai our God, Ruler of the universe, who creates many different spices.

Baruch Atah, Adonai,
Eloheinu, Melech ha'olam,
borei minei v'samim.

בָּרוּךְ אַתָּה, יְיָ,
אֱלֹהֵינוּ, מֶלֶךְ הָעוֹלָם,
בּוֹרֵא מִינֵי בְשָׂמִים.

RAISE THE WINE GLASSES AND RECITE:

We drink a cup of wine in celebration of that ordinary life.

Blessed are You, Adonai our God, Ruler of the universe, who creates the fruit of the vine.

Baruch Atah, Adonai
Eloheinu, Melech ha'olam,
borei p'ri hagafen.

בָּרוּךְ אַתָּה, יְיָ,
אֱלֹהֵינוּ, מֶלֶךְ הָעוֹלָם,
בּוֹרֵא פְּרִי הַגָּפֶן.

L'chayim! To life!

DRINK THE WINE.

Consider: It is natural to believe that shadows are fleeting, that trouble will pass quickly, and that someone else will take care of the world's problems. How can we tell if danger is growing or fading?

5

TROUBLES · צָרוֹת

We must be watchful. When we ignore the rising shadows of hatred, they engulf us.

We remember:

Hatred spread across Germany like poison in water.

The Germans afflicted us with cruel laws and humiliations. They did not care who we were or what we did. They did not care whether we were religious or secular, from the city or from the country, civilian or soldier, only that we were Jews.

The Psalms reflect our anguish: "Every day they make my words sorrowful; all their thoughts about me are for evil. They gather and hide; they watch my steps; they hope to capture my soul." (Psalms 56:6–7)

Trouble begins not with a fanfare, but as storm clouds building in the distance.

We remember:

"Every day they keep issuing new laws against Jews. Today for example, they took all our appliances away from us: the sewing machine, the radio, the telephone, the vacuum cleaner, the electric fryer, my camera, and my bicycle. . . . Agi said we should be happy they're taking things and not people." (**Éva Heyman**, Holocaust victim, Romania)

In the overcrowded ghettos, we lamented, "I feel as if I am in a box. There is no air to breathe. Wherever you go, you encounter a gate that hems you in. I feel as if I have been robbed, my freedom is being robbed from me, my home, and the familiar streets I love so much. I have been cut off from all that is dear and precious to me." (**Yitzkhok Rudashevski**, Holocaust victim, Lithuania)

Many European Jews fought for their countries in World War I, but their service did not protect them from the Holocaust.

Rear Entrance, Terezin Ghetto, 1941-1944,
Bedřich Fritta, India ink and wash on paper

THE TEARS OF THE GHETTO

DIP A POTATO SKIN INTO SALT WATER.

These potato skins remind us that in the deprivation of the ghetto, we ate whatever we could find. The salt water in which we dip them recalls our tears.

RECITE:

We dip to remember our starvation, evoking the salt of our tears and the hardships we endured.

> Blessed are You, Adonai our God, Ruler of the universe,
> who creates the fruit of the earth.

> *Baruch Atah, Adonai*   בָּרוּךְ אַתָּה, יְיָ
> *Eloheinu, Melech ha'olam,* אֱלֹהֵינוּ, מֶלֶךְ הָעוֹלָם,
> *borei p'ri ha'adamah.*   בּוֹרֵא פְּרִי הָאֲדָמָה.

EAT THE POTATO SKIN.

KIDDUSH IN THE GHETTO

We remember:

> Even in the ghetto, we celebrated Shabbat. We found, however, that wine for Kiddush was often impossible to get. The rabbis ruled that sweet tea could be substituted.

RAISE THE TEA GLASSES AND RECITE:

We drink this tea in memory of the Kiddush wine we could not have.

> Blessed are You, Adonai our God, Ruler of the universe,
> by whose word everything comes into being.

> *Baruch Atah, Adonai*   בָּרוּךְ אַתָּה, יְיָ
> *Eloheinu, Melech ha'olam,* אֱלֹהֵינוּ, מֶלֶךְ הָעוֹלָם,
> *shehakol nih'yeh bid'varo.* שֶׁהַכֹּל נִהְיֶה בִּדְבָרוֹ.

DRINK THE TEA.

HIDING · הַחְבָּאָה

We remember:

Holding on to the hope that we might one day be reunited, we sent our children into hiding. A few were sent to safety beyond the borders. Others found hiding places with friends, neighbors, and strangers.

"As Mommy and Omi waved to me, I chose to hide my tears, and I smiled. I wanted to give them strength." (**Ruth Siegel Westheimer**, Holocaust orphan, Germany)

CONCEALMENT

HOLD UP THE CHILD'S DRAWING.

This drawing represents our hope for our children and our faith in their future. Hope and faith may seem frail comfort, but they are steel girders that give us the strength to stand.

As we did in the time of trouble, we now conceal our hope in a secret place to keep it safe. May we find it again at the end of our journey.

HAND THE DRAWING TO A PARTICIPANT.

Hide our hope. Protect this picture until we are once again safe, and we can reveal our hope and our faith to the world.

HIDE THE DRAWING IN A SAFE PLACE FROM WHERE IT CAN EASILY BE RETRIEVED.

Consider: Thousands of children were hidden with non-Jewish families, in convents, and in orphanages. Many children in hiding spent the entire war pretending to be someone they were not. How does a child reclaim an identity they have all but lost? Why might they not want to do so?

HIDDEN SWEETNESS

Hope can be a sweetness that lies beneath bitterness: hope for our children's future, that we would see them again, that this horror would end.

TAKE A PIECE OF ORANGE AND RECITE:

We eat this orange, whose bitter rind hides sweet fruit, to remember that sweet hope can hide beneath bitterness.

Blessed are You, Adonai our God, Ruler of the universe, who creates the fruit of the tree.

*Baruch Atah, Adonai
Eloheinu, Melech ha'olam,
borei p'ri ha'eitz.*

בָּרוּךְ אַתָּה, יְיָ
אֱלֹהֵינוּ, מֶלֶךְ הָעוֹלָם,
בּוֹרֵא פְּרִי הָעֵץ.

EAT THE ORANGE.

"For two years, we lived with them. For two years, I did not leave the building. For two years, I did not walk around the apartment. For two years, I did not go near a window—I would always crawl underneath."

(Hannah Gofrit, Holocaust survivor, Poland)

TERROR · אֵימָה

Words fail as we begin to speak of the darkest times.

We remember:

The Germans, with willing partners, murdered us in staggering numbers. Mass graves filled the forests of Europe.

"My heart shudders within me, and the terrors of death have descended upon me. Fear and trembling penetrate me, and I am enveloped with horror." (Psalms 55:5–6)

We were murdered without mercy: mothers and fathers, children and grandparents. We were murdered simply for being Jews.

The Germans forced us from our homes into ghettos, into slave labor camps, and into death chambers.

"In our blind ignorance, we thought that deportation was a better solution. Fools that we were, we thought that the ghetto was the ultimate in abysmal blackness. We did not know that from here on, we would be severed and cut off from everything that was familiar and dear to us. We did not know that from that train ride on, we would be robbed of our whole world." (**Sara Selver-Urbach**, Holocaust survivor, Poland)

Winter, 1944, Zinovii Tolkatchev
charcoal and crayon on paper

Consider: Some people gave up opportunities to escape in order to stay with elderly parents, young children, or other family members. Why would someone make such a choice?

THE LOST COMMUNITIES

REFILL THE WINE CUPS. DO NOT DRINK.

We grieve as we remember the vibrant Jewish communities that were destroyed.

"A cry is heard in Ramah—wailing, bitter weeping— Rachel weeping for her children. She refuses to be comforted for her children who are gone."
(Jeremiah 31:14)

READ TOGETHER:

> We spill drops of wine to remember the blood that was spilled, the whole communities that were destroyed. These losses diminish our lives as we diminish the wine in our glasses.
>
> Let these few represent for us the many.

These names represent the range of Jewish communities that existed before the war: small and large, traditional and modern, Ashkenazi and Sephardi. Some were completely destroyed; others remain, though smaller than before

[See page 36 for more information about these lost communities.]

DIP A FINGER IN THE WINE AND SPILL A DROP FOR EACH COMMUNITY, RECITING THE NAMES TOGETHER.

WARSAW (**wawr**-saw)	SARAJEVO (sar-uh-**yey**-voh)
VIENNA (vee-**en**-uh)	CHELM (**khelm**–that's a guttural **kh**)
SALONIKA (sal-uh-**nee**-kuh)	KIELCE (**kyel**-tse)
RIGA (**ree**-guh)	WIESBADEN (**vees**-bahd-n)
KIEV (**kee**-ev)	PRAGUE (**prahg**)

OPTIONAL: ASK FOR NAMES OF ADDITIONAL COMMUNITIES. AS EACH NAME IS GIVEN, REPEAT THE NAME AND SPILL A DROP OF WINE.

FROM DARKNESS INTO LIGHT

We pause in terror before the human deed
The cloud of annihilation, the concentration of death
The cruelly casual way of each to each.
But in the stillness of this hour,
We find our way from darkness into light.
(**Chaim Stern**)

11

STRENGTH · כֹּחַ

We remember:

Despite our enemies' eagerness to strip us of our Judaism and of our humanity, we continued to educate our children, to celebrate our holidays, to love and help each other.

Although prayer was forbidden, we prayed in secret communities and within the secret places in our hearts. "Our faith was the one thing they could not take from us." (**Rivka Wagner**, Holocaust survivor, Poland)

Hidden between the bunks, we whispered the familiar words of the Friday evening prayers and found tranquility. "I discovered for the first time in my life the real power and value of prayer and faith in God. I could feel my words shattering the iron gates and the high-powered fences, going past the hundreds of guards, dugouts, and watchtowers, out into the open, reaching toward heaven. Here, I knew, was a way of escape, a source of strength, and a means of survival of which no power on earth could deprive me." (**Simcha Unsdorfer**, Holocaust survivor, Czechoslovakia)

In the ghetto, a young boy defied the bitterness.

Camp Synagogue in Saint Cyprien, 1941,
Felix Nussbaum, oil on plywood

FROM TOMORROW ON

From tomorrow on, I shall be sad—
From tomorrow on.
Today I will be happy.

What's the use of sadness—tell me that?
Because the evil winds begin to blow?
Why should I grieve for tomorrow—
today?

No, today I will be glad.

And every day, no matter how bitter it be,
I will say:
From tomorrow on, I shall be sad—
Not today.

(**Motele**, a child in the ghetto,
excerpted)

Many have tried to destroy us: Pharaoh, Amalek, Haman, Caesar, the Inquisition, the Nazis. None have succeeded. In the Torah, we are commanded, "Choose life, so that you and your children shall live." (Deuteronomy 30:19)

READ TOGETHER:

"As long as that secret power is concealed within us, we shall not yield to despair." (**Chaim Kaplan**, Holocaust victim, Poland)

As we fight physical, mental, and spiritual battles, we cry out the generations-old refrain, "L'chayim! To life!" We continue to live our Judaism and not let the evil destroy our faith in God or in humanity.

"Today the ghetto celebrated the circulation of the hundred thousandth book in the ghetto library. . . . Hundreds of people read in the ghetto. The reading of books in the ghetto is the greatest pleasure for me. The book unites us with the future; the book unites us with the world." (**Yitzkhok Rudashevski**, Holocaust victim, Lithuania)

THE UNBREAKABLE CORE

HOLD UP THE FRUIT AND RECITE TOGETHER:

These fruits, with their unbreakable inner core, represent our inner strength. They are a tangible token of the power to resist. We eat these fruits so that we may gain courage from our ancestors to find our own inner strength in difficult times.

Blessed are You, Adonai our God, Ruler of the universe, who creates the fruit of the tree.

Baruch Atah, Adonai Eloheinu, Melech ha'olam, borei p'ri ha'eitz.

בָּרוּךְ אַתָּה, יְיָ
אֱלֹהֵינוּ, מֶלֶךְ הָעוֹלָם,
בּוֹרֵא פְּרִי הָעֵץ.

EAT THE FRUIT.

Consider: How has the injunction to "choose life" helped us to survive in difficult times? What does "choose life" mean when life feels truly impossible?

HELP · עֶזְרָה

"I do not know what a Jew is; we only know what human beings are." (**Pastor André Trocmé**, Holocaust rescuer, France)

How do we stay hopeful when people are capable of such great evil?

A few good people recognized the evil for what it was. They risked their lives to help us. They hid friends, neighbors, and strangers from the eyes of those who would harm us. In almost every survivor's story, there is a story of someone who helped.

We remember:

Helpers lived in every country in Europe. They came from every walk of life. Some saved hundreds. Some saved one. They saved as many as they could, regretting only that they didn't save more.

Having been their nanny for thirteen years, twenty-six-year-old Erzsebet Fajo swore she would protect the Abonyi family. As the bombs fell on Budapest and the fascist militias searched the streets for Jews, Erzsebet risked her life daily to find a safe place for each family member to hide. "She saved us day by day." (**Zsuzsanna Abonyi Ozsváth**, Holocaust survivor, Hungary)

With her partners at the secret organization Żegota, Irena Sendler smuggled thousands of Jewish children out of the Warsaw Ghetto. She hid them in ambulances, snuck them through underground passageways, and wheeled them out concealed in boxes and suitcases. She kept track of the children on papers buried in glass bottles, hoping someday to reunite them with their families. "Every child saved with my help is the justification of my existence on this earth, and not a title to glory." (**Irena Sendler**, Holocaust rescuer, Poland)

Żegota was an underground resistance organization run by the Polish government-in-exile. The organization provided food, medical care, money, and forged documents to Jews throughout Poland.

Liberation,
Shmuel Leitner

We honor the helpers so that we may gain wisdom from them. We must always strive for the courage to help those in need.

RISE AND GRASP THE WRIST OF ANOTHER PARTICIPANT. READ TOGETHER:

We stand hand to wrist as if pulling each other to safety.

Each person's decision to help was difficult. The risks were many. Would we have made such a decision? We cannot know. We cannot judge.

In gratitude and hope, we honor the helpers. We draw inspiration from them and vow to never be indifferent to the plight of others. Strength comes to those who pursue justice.

RELEASE HANDS AND BE SEATED.

"We must know these good people who helped Jews during the Holocaust. We must learn from them, and in gratitude and hope, we must remember them." **(Elie Wiesel**, Holocaust survivor, Hungary)

RESOLVE · נְחִישׁוּת

We remember:

Liberation eventually came. As the armies of the world moved toward vanquishing evil, they discovered a hell that left them stunned.

"It will be a time of trouble, as has never been before. At that time, your people will be rescued." (Daniel 12:1)

READ TOGETHER:

We must remember the affliction of our people so that no people shall ever suffer such a fate again.

We are commanded to provide comfort wherever there is suffering, "for you know the heart of the stranger, since you were strangers in the land of Egypt." (Exodus 23:9)

NEVER AGAIN

READ RESPONSIVELY:

How do we ensure that no one ever suffers such a fate again?

We resolve to strengthen the world through our commitment to justice.
We say: *L'olam lo od.* Never again.

Never again shall we ignore the gathering shadows of hate.

L'olam lo od.   לְעוֹלָם לֹא עוֹד.

Never again shall we stay silent at the preaching of malice.

L'olam lo od.   לְעוֹלָם לֹא עוֹד.

Never again shall we excuse those who hate.

L'olam lo od.   לְעוֹלָם לֹא עוֹד.

Blessed are You, Adonai our God, Ruler of the universe,
who girds Israel with strength.

Baruch Atah, Adonai Eloheinu, Melech ha'olam, ozeir Yisrael big'vurah.   בָּרוּךְ אַתָּה, יְיָ אֱלֹהֵינוּ, מֶלֶךְ הָעוֹלָם, אוֹזֵר יִשְׂרָאֵל בִּגְבוּרָה.

To the Man who Restored my Belief in Humanity, 1945, Yehuda Bacon, gouache, black chalk and pencil on paper

Never again shall we stand and watch while people are mistreated.

L'olam lo od. לְעוֹלָם לֹא עוֹד.

Never again shall we allow groups of people to be separated and made unequal.

L'olam lo od. לְעוֹלָם לֹא עוֹד.

Never again shall we watch a community plant the seeds of hate and do nothing.

L'olam lo od. לְעוֹלָם לֹא עוֹד.

Blessed are You, Adonai our God, Ruler of the universe, who frees the captive.

Baruch Atah, Adonai Eloheinu, בָּרוּךְ אַתָּה, יְיָ אֱלֹהֵינוּ,
Melech ha'olam, matir asurim. מֶלֶךְ הָעוֹלָם, מַתִּיר אֲסוּרִים.

Never again shall we think we are helpless to stop the coming of evil.

L'olam lo od. לְעוֹלָם לֹא עוֹד.

Never again shall we forget our own strength.

L'olam lo od. לְעוֹלָם לֹא עוֹד.

Never again shall we allow hatred to go unanswered.

L'olam lo od. לְעוֹלָם לֹא עוֹד.

Blessed are You, Adonai our God, Ruler of the universe, who commands us to pursue justice.

Baruch Atah, Adonai Eloheinu, בָּרוּךְ אַתָּה, יְיָ אֱלֹהֵינוּ,
Melech ha'olam, asher kid'shanu מֶלֶךְ הָעוֹלָם, אֲשֶׁר קִדְּשָׁנוּ
b'mitzvotav v'tzivanu lirdof tzedek. בְּמִצְוֹתָיו וְצִוָּנוּ לִרְדוֹף צֶדֶק.

LIFE · חַיִּים

A question stands stark before us: How do we move forward when we have lost so much?

READ TOGETHER:

> We walk with a hole in our hearts and weight in our footsteps, but we walk forward. We are reduced, but we refuse to remain broken.

One Spring, 1941, Karl Robert Bodek and Kurt Conard Löw
watercolor, India ink and pencil on paper

We remember:

> While the world counted their dead, we counted our living. Those who lived gave us strength to love again.
>
> In a displaced persons camp near Munich, Frania Bratt married Boris Blum five months after liberation. Their hand-printed wedding invitations listed both their hometowns and the death camps they had survived. Their daughter Towa was one of many babies born in the camp that year.
>
> We did not know what would come next. We only knew we could not go back to the life we once lived.
>
> We brought our children, and our hope, out of hiding.

RETURN THE CHILD'S DRAWING TO THE TABLE.

THE HOPE

Let us once again restore hope and joy openly to our lives. Let us now return the drawing, a symbol of our hope for our children, to the table.

We remember:

> As we emerged from the rubble of our lives, we were united by an ancient hope. "Hatikvah," the expression of that hope, is a song that has bolstered us in times of joy and in times of sorrow. It was the clarion call when we dreamed of a better life, a life of freedom and a land of our own, even while trapped in slavery.

"Hatikvah" is the anthem of the State of Israel, but Jews sang it long before the establishment of the state. The text was written in 1878 by Naphtali Imber, a Polish Jewish poet. The melody is generally attributed to Samuel Cohen in 1888, based on a Romanian folk song he heard as a child.

STAND AND SING:

As long as the Jewish spirit is yearning deep in the heart,
With eyes turned toward the East, looking toward Zion,
Then our hope, the two-thousand-year-old hope, will not be lost:
To be a free people in our land, the Land of Zion and Jerusalem.

Kol od baleivav p'nimah,	כָּל עוֹד בַּלֵּבָב פְּנִימָה,
nefesh Yehudi homiyah,	נֶפֶשׁ יְהוּדִי הוֹמִיָּה,
Ul'fa'atei mizrach kadimah,	וּלְפַאֲתֵי מִזְרָח קָדִימָה,
ayin l'Tziyon tzofiyah,	עַיִן לְצִיּוֹן צוֹפִיָּה,
Od lo avdah tikvateinu,	עוֹד לֹא אָבְדָה תִּקְוָתֵנוּ,
hatikvah bat sh'not alpayim:	הַתִּקְוָה בַּת שְׁנוֹת אַלְפַּיִם:
Lih'yot am chofshi b'artzeinu,	לִהְיוֹת עַם חָפְשִׁי בְּאַרְצֵנוּ,
Eretz Tziyon virushalayim.	אֶרֶץ צִיּוֹן וִירוּשָׁלָיִם.

CELEBRATING OUR SURVIVAL

With hope in our hearts, we step out of the darkness and into the light of renewed life.

READ TOGETHER:

As we were all at Sinai, so we are all the children of survivors.

As it is written in the Torah, "And you shall tell your child on that day, 'It is because of what Adonai did for me when I went free from Egypt.'" (Exodus 13:8)

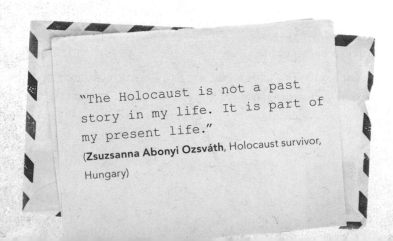

"The Holocaust is not a past story in my life. It is part of my present life."
(**Zsuzsanna Abonyi Ozsváth**, Holocaust survivor, Hungary)

RECITE:

We say the Shehecheyanu to give thanks that we have made it to this time and place. We say it here because although much was lost, we survived, and that survival is worthy of celebration. We drink a cup of wine to celebrate our rebirth.

Blessed are You, Adonai our God, Ruler of the universe, who has supported us, protected us, and brought us to this moment.

Baruch Atah, Adonai	בָּרוּךְ אַתָּה, יְיָ
Eloheinu, Melech ha'olam,	אֱלֹהֵינוּ, מֶלֶךְ הָעוֹלָם,
shehecheyanu, v'kiy'manu,	שֶׁהֶחֱיָנוּ וְקִיְּמָנוּ,
v'higi'anu laz'man hazeh.	וְהִגִּיעָנוּ לַזְּמַן הַזֶּה.

RAISE THE WINE GLASSES AND RECITE:

Blessed are You, Adonai our God, Ruler of the universe, who creates the fruit of the vine.

Baruch Atah, Adonai	בָּרוּךְ אַתָּה, יְיָ
Eloheinu, Melech ha'olam,	אֱלֹהֵינוּ, מֶלֶךְ הָעוֹלָם,
borei p'ri hagafen.	בּוֹרֵא פְּרִי הַגָּפֶן.

L'chayim! To life!

DRINK THE WINE.

MEMORY · זִכָּרוֹן

Our joy in our survival is tempered by the tears for those we lost. They left no footprints, no fingerprints. All we have is memory.

READ TOGETHER:

> In this moment, we acknowledge that they lived. As long as we remember them, they are with us.

THEY ARE GONE

They are gone.
They cannot tell their stories any longer.
But we can.
We can hold open the window, this fragile window,
We can give their stories wings.
Let us give their stories a voice, so they can fly into
others' ears, into others' hearts.
Only we can tell their stories now.
Only we.
(**Jennifer Zunikoff**)

The survivors entreat us, "I ask you not to forget the dead. I ask you to build a memorial in our names, a monument reaching up to the heavens, that the entire world might see. Not a monument of marble or stone, but one of good deeds. I believe with full and perfect faith that only such a monument can promise a better future. Only thus can we be sure that the evil that overturned the world and turned our lives into hell will never return." (Adapted from **Donia Rosen**, Holocaust survivor, Ukraine)

Taleskoten, 1944, Zinovii Tolkatchev
gouache, charcoal and crayon on paper

THE LOST

Let us remember them as they lived. As we contemplate their pictures, we mourn the stories cut short, the hopes and dreams lost. We speak their names, so they will not be forgotten.

Some people in these photos are not named, reminding us that although some stories are lost, we still acknowledge the people who lived them. For these, we simply say, "unknown."

The Nazis targeted a number of non-Jewish groups, including gay men, people with mental disabilities, political dissidents, and the Romani ethnic group, European nomads derogatorily known as gypsies. The Romani call the Holocaust the Porajmos, which means "the devouring." Almost 50 percent of European Romani were murdered in the Porajmos.

RISE AND READ THE NAMES NEXT TO THE PHOTOS ON THE FOLLOWING PAGES.
OPTIONAL: ASK PARTICIPANTS FOR ADDITIONAL NAMES OF VICTIMS.

Florika Liebmann   Bela Rodnianski   Boris Tzeitin   Maria Tzeitin   Unknown

Hannah Joskowitz   Zhunia Joskowitz   Gabor Neuman   Joseph Broudo   Zvi Segal

23

Henryk Szwarc — Aron Goldman Bodner — Mara Coblic — Margarete Jacoby — Heinrich Jacoby

Elly Weisz — Helga Hamm — Artur Rubin — Truda Rubin — Wiliam Wolf Zeev Kohn

Let us pause for a moment of silent reflection.

TAKE A MOMENT OF SILENCE.

I AM WITH YOU STILL

I give you this one thought to keep:
I am with you still, I do not sleep.

I am a thousand winds that blow,
I am the diamond glints on snow,
I am the sunlight on ripened grain,
I am the gentle autumn rain.

When you awaken
In the morning's hush,
I am the sweet uplifting rush
Of quiet birds in circled flight.
I am the soft stars that shine at night.

Do not think of me as gone,
I am with you still in each new dawn.

(**Mary Elizabeth Frye**, adapted)

KADDISH

REMAIN STANDING. LIGHT THE *YAHRTZEIT* CANDLE(S).

We did not die alone. We say Kaddish not only for our own dead, but also for the many who were targeted alongside us—Romani people, gay people, those with disabilities, and voices of resistance—all murdered in the great silencing of diversity, speech, and opposition. We feel their loss as we gather and mourn our own, immeasurable losses.

RECITE:

Yitgadal v'yitkadash sh'mei raba	יִתְגַּדַּל וְיִתְקַדַּשׁ שְׁמֵהּ רַבָּא
B'alma di v'ra chir'utei,	בְּעָלְמָא דִּי בְרָא כִרְעוּתֵהּ,
v'yamlich malchutei	וְיַמְלִיךְ מַלְכוּתֵהּ
b'chayeichon uv'yomeichon uv'chayei	בְּחַיֵּיכוֹן וּבְיוֹמֵיכוֹן וּבְחַיֵּי
d'chol beit Yisrael,	דְכָל בֵּית יִשְׂרָאֵל,
ba'agala uviz'man kariv.	בַּעֲגָלָא וּבִזְמַן קָרִיב.
V'imru: Amen.	וְאִמְרוּ: אָמֵן.
Y'hei sh'mei raba m'varach l'alam	יְהֵא שְׁמֵהּ רַבָּא מְבָרַךְ לְעָלַם
ul'almei almaya.	וּלְעָלְמֵי עָלְמַיָּא.
Yitbarach v'yishtabach v'yitpa'ar	יִתְבָּרַךְ וְיִשְׁתַּבַּח וְיִתְפָּאַר
v'yitromam v'yitnasei,	וְיִתְרוֹמַם וְיִתְנַשֵּׂא
v'yit'hadar v'yit'aleh v'yit'halal sh'mei	וְיִתְהַדָּר וְיִתְעַלֶּה וְיִתְהַלָּל שְׁמֵהּ
d'Kud'sha, B'rich Hu,	דְּקֻדְשָׁא, בְּרִיךְ הוּא,
l'eila min kol birchata v'shirata	לְעֵלָּא מִן כָּל בִּרְכָתָא וְשִׁירָתָא
tushb'chata v'nechemata	תֻּשְׁבְּחָתָא וְנֶחֱמָתָא
da'amiran b'alma. V'imru: Amen.	דַּאֲמִירָן בְּעָלְמָא. וְאִמְרוּ: אָמֵן.
Y'hei sh'lama raba min sh'maya	יְהֵא שְׁלָמָה רַבָּא מִן שְׁמַיָּא
v'chayim aleinu, v'al kol Yisrael.	וְחַיִּים עָלֵינוּ, וְעַל כָּל יִשְׂרָאֵל.
V'imru: Amen.	וְאִמְרוּ: אָמֵן.
Oseh shalom bimromav, Hu ya'aseh	עוֹשֶׂה שָׁלוֹם בִּמְרוֹמָיו, הוּא יַעֲשֶׂה
shalom aleinu, v'al kol Yisrael.	שָׁלוֹם עָלֵינוּ, וְעַל כָּל יִשְׂרָאֵל.
V'imru: Amen.	וְאִמְרוּ: אָמֵן.

May the One who brings peace around the world bring peace to all of us
and to all who mourn. Amen.

COMMUNITY · קְהִלָּה

We remember:

> In the starving times, we dreamed of cooking in the kitchens of home. In the aftermath, when we contemplated all that had been lost, it was the recipes of those lost kitchens that comforted us.

> We reached out and touched nothing,
> So we turned inward instead.
> Our memories kept us moving forward,
> Our memories of home and of bread.

> We cannot return home, it's rubble.
> We cannot hold family, they're gone.
> But today, today we will have dumplings,
> And tomorrow, we will live on.

> **(Violet Neff-Helms)**

From the abundance of our brightest lives to the sharing of scraps in the darkest times, communities rise with the sharing of bread. Our ancestors understood this: "Let all who are hungry come and eat. Let all who are needy, come and celebrate with us." (Passover haggadah) Let us take up that call, to share our friendship with all who are in need.

Consider: Several cookbooks written by women in the ghettos or camps have survived. Why would starving people spend their time recording recipes they could not follow?

HOLD UP THE BREAD AND RECITE:

As we break bread together, we give thanks for our survival, acknowledging that we are no more deserving than those who did not survive.

We celebrate the Jewish community that continues to thrive and the community we have created between us here today.

> **Blessed are You, Adonai our God, Ruler of the universe,
> who brings forth bread from the earth.**

Baruch Atah, Adonai	בָּרוּךְ אַתָּה, יְיָ
Eloheinu, Melech ha'olam,	אֱלֹהֵינוּ, מֶלֶךְ הָעוֹלָם,
hamotzi lechem	הַמּוֹצִיא לֶחֶם
min ha'aretz.	מִן הָאָרֶץ.

EAT THE BREAD.

AWAKENING · הִתְעוֹרְרוּת

KNOCK ON THE TABLE SEVERAL TIMES.

"Awaken, awaken, put on your strength, O Zion." (Isaiah 52:1)

We awaken to a world where human beings have done unfathomable evil to each other, to us. What do we do now?

We weep and ask: How do we go on living after such a loss?

We are commanded to choose life. We remember that our ancestors held on to love and life and hope, even in the harshest times. We know that the thread of Jewish life is strong. As survivors say, "Grandchildren are the best revenge."

Overwhelmed by the enormity of the story, we whisper: I do not want to hear any more.

We draw inward to comfort one another, and yet we know: ignoring evil only allows it to grow. Despite our unease, we choose not to be blind. We choose awareness because we recognize that "evil does not need our help, just our indifference." (Adapted from **Hanns Loewenbach**, Holocaust refugee, Germany to America)

We cry out in anger: How could this happen? Where was the world?

We remember not only the evil of those who hurt us, but also the goodness of those few who helped us. We resolve to turn our anger into a passionate drive to repair the world.

Awakened, we inquire: How does hatred grow? Can we stop it?

Hatred grows when we ignore it, when we allow hateful behavior to go unchallenged. We will not let evil hide in the shadows. We resolve to shine a spotlight on hate and make it clear that such behavior is not acceptable. We will be vocal torchbearers of love.

*View of Buchenwald,
a Few Days After
Liberation*, 1945,
Jakob Zim, watercolor
on paper

AN AFFIRMATION FOR THE FUTURE

READ RESPONSIVELY:

I pray for courage, and for strength.
When I remember the evils in the past,
The innocent people tortured and murdered,
I am almost afraid to make myself remember.
But I am even more afraid to forget.

> I ask for wisdom, that I might mourn,
> And not be consumed by hatred.
> That I might remember,
> And yet not lose hope.

I must face evil—
And, so doing, reaffirm my faith in future good.
I cannot erase yesterday's pains,
But I can vow that they will not have suffered in vain.

> And so I pray:
> For those who were given death, I choose life
> For me and for generations yet to come.

For those who found courage to stand against evil—
Often at the cost of their lives—
I vow to carry on their struggle.

> I must teach myself, and others
> to learn from hatred that people must love,
> to learn from evil to live for good.

In days past, a *schulklopfer*
(a synagogue knocker)
would go door to door,
knocking four times at each
door, to awaken the people
for prayers. In some parts
of Europe, *schulklopfers*
used a particular pattern,
knock–pause
knock, knock
pause–knock.

PEACE & JUSTICE · צֶדֶק

READ RESPONSIVELY:

We recognize that despite our best efforts, there is still evil in the world. People are still persecuted for who they are. Anger and hatred continue to seep into our communities.

> Nonetheless, we proclaim that there is hope. We can make a difference. We can help.

"Without justice, there can be no peace. He who passively accepts evil is as much involved in it as he who helps to perpetrate it." (**Martin Luther King Jr.**)

> To stem the flow of hatred, we must work for justice. "For the work of justice shall be peace." (Isaiah 32:17)

WORDS OF PEACE

Across this world, we are many different people. We speak many different languages. Peace is a gift we can give in every language.

READ WORDS OF PEACE ALOUD.

Salám	ARABIC	سلام	Heiwa	JAPANESE	平和
Shalom	HEBREW	שלום	Eirini	GREEK	Ειρήνη
Mir	RUSSIAN	Мир	Pyonghwa	KOREAN	평화
Frithur	ICELANDIC	Friður	Asiti	KURDISH	هاسیتی
Freeden	GERMAN	Frieden	Meero	ROMANI	Miro
Santiphap	KHMER	សន្តិភាព	Pache	ITALIAN	Pace
Pay	FRENCH	Paix	Samaya	SINHALESE	සමය
Shaanti	HINDI	शांति	Bizaanizi	OJIBWE	Bizaanizi

TO WORK FOR PEACE AND JUSTICE

We cannot change our past, but we can build our future.

"Do not be daunted by the enormity of the world's grief. Do justly, now. Love *chesed*, now. Walk humbly, now. You are not obligated to complete the work, but neither are you free to abandon it." (**Rami Shapiro**)

We must remember that peace and justice are not gifts from God. They are our gifts to each other. (Adapted from **Elie Wiesel**, Holocaust survivor, Hungary)

RECITE TOGETHER:

We pledge ourselves to work for peace and justice throughout the world.

Justice, justice we shall pursue.
(Adapted from Deuteronomy 16:20)

Tzedek, tzedek nirdof.   צֶדֶק, צֶדֶק נִרְדֹּף.

Consider: How can we work for justice in our community or among our friends and family? How can working for justice in our community make a difference in the world as a whole?

STORIES

STORIES OF THE HOLOCAUST VICTIMS, SURVIVORS, FIGHTERS, AND RESCUERS WHOSE WORDS AND ARTWORK APPEAR IN THIS BOOK:

Robert Antelme was part of a resistance group in France led by François Mitterand. He was deported to Buchenwald in 1944. On liberation, Mitterand pulled the living Antelme from a pile of dead bodies.

Yehuda Bacon was born in 1929 in Czechoslovakia. In 1942, he was sent to Terezin and then to Auschwitz. His sketches of the crematoria and gas chambers served as testimony at the Eichmann trial. He immigrated to Israel, where he joined the faculty of the Bezalel Academy of Art.

Frania and **Boris Blum** met and married in a displaced persons camp in 1945. Having survived the deprivations of the ghetto, camps, and continued antisemitism, the young Jewish couple immigrated with their daughter to the United States in 1959 and settled in Brooklyn, New York. The simple hand-sewn dress Frania had made in celebration of liberation became a symbol of hope throughout her life.

Karl Robert Bodek and **Kurt Conrad Löw** often collaborated on their artwork. Together, they prepared stage settings for the cabaret at the Gurs internment camp in France. Bodek was transported to Drancy and Auschwitz, where he was murdered. Löw was released and made his way to Geneva. He returned to Vienna, his birthplace, in 1952, where he lived until his death in 1980.

Dr. Susan Cernyak-Spatz was born in Berlin in 1929. Fleeing the Nazis across Europe, she and her family were eventually deported to Terezin and then to Auschwitz. After liberation, she worked as an interpreter for the American Counter-Intelligence Corps. She became a professor in the Department of Language and Culture Studies at the University of North Carolina at Charlotte.

Erzsebet Fajo was thirteen years old when she came to work for the Abonyi family in 1931. In 1944, when the family was in danger, she risked her life to save them. After the war, the Abonyis adopted her and paid for her education. She was recognized by Yad Vashem as "Righteous Among the Nations" in 1986.

Bedřich Fritta was a graphic designer and cartoonist in Prague. As director of the painting section of the Technical Department at the Terezin Ghetto, he was forced to provide propaganda material for the Germans. In secret, Fritta and his colleagues smuggled out paintings depicting the horrors of ghetto life. After these were discovered, Fritta was sent to Auschwitz, where he died.

Hannah Gofrit was born in 1935 in Biała Rawska, Poland. She spent the war hiding with her mother in the Warsaw home of non-Jewish friends. In 1949, she moved to Israel, where she became the chief nurse in Tel Aviv's Public Health Division.

Éva Heyman turned thirteen in 1944. Three days later she was deported to Auschwitz and eventually murdered. Her mother, Agi, survived the war but committed suicide in 1949.

Chaim Kaplan was born in Horodyszcze, Belarus, in 1880. In 1902, he moved to Warsaw to help found a pioneering elementary Hebrew school and was principal there for forty years. His diary was smuggled out of the ghetto and survived the war. He and his wife are believed to have been murdered in Treblinka in 1942.

Shmuel Leitner spent his teenage years shuttling among seven different concentration camps. At each one, he drew what he witnessed, using scraps of paper such as cement bags as his canvas. Each time he was moved to a new camp, his art was destroyed, and he would re-create it again and again. He survived and later moved to Israel. He rediscovered his brother in Poland after 40 years, each believing the other had perished.

Hanns Loewenbach was born in Germany in 1915. He escaped to Italy and then settled in China with his parents. After the war, he moved to the United States, where he lived until his death in 2012. He is survived by his three children and six grandchildren.

Felix Nussbaum was born in Osnabrueck, Germany, and settled in Belgium in 1935. In 1940, Felix was arrested and sent to the Saint Cyprien internment camp in southern France. He escaped and lived in hiding in Brussels until he was caught in 1944 and sent to Auschwitz, where he was murdered.

Dr. Zsuzsanna Abonyi Ozsváth was born in 1931 in Hungary. She survived the war with the help of the family's nanny, Erzsebet Fajo. She became the director of Holocaust Studies at the University of Texas at Dallas.

Donia Rosen was born in Kosov, Galicia. She was twelve when she hid in the forest after her family was murdered. She survived with the help of Olena Hryhoryszyn, an elderly non-Jewish friend. She immigrated to Israel in 1948.

Yitzkhok Rudashevski was born in 1927 in Vilna, Poland. He and his parents were murdered in the killing pit at Ponary in 1943. His cousin discovered his diary when, after the war, she returned to the hiding place their families had shared.

Pierre Sauvage (see Discussion Guide) is a French/American documentary filmmaker. He was born to a Jewish family in 1944 in Le Chambon, France, a town where the local people hid and protected Jews.

Sara Selver-Urbach was born in 1923 in Łódź, Poland. She wrote her diary on the backs of used vouchers in the office of the forced labor camp where she worked. She survived the war and moved to Israel.

Irena Sendler was a Polish social worker and the head of the children's section of Żegota, an underground resistance organization. She saved thousands of children from the Warsaw Ghetto. She lived in Warsaw until her death at age ninety-eight in 2008. She was recognized by Yad Vashem as "Righteous Among the Nations" in 1965.

Hannah Senesh was a poet whose work has become an integral part of modern Jewish liturgy. She was born in Hungary and moved to Palestine in 1939. In 1944, at the age of twenty-two, she parachuted into Hungary as a member of the Jewish paramilitary Haganah assisting the British army. She was captured and executed.

Zinovii Tolkatchev was a Jew and a member of the Russian armed forces that liberated Majdanek and Auschwitz. Many of his drawings from the liberation of Auschwitz were done on the commandant's personal stationary and include the words *Kommandantur Konzentrationslager Auschwitz* in bold black letters.

Pastor André Trocmé urged his congregation to give shelter to any Jew who should ask for it. With his wife, Magda, he created a haven for persecuted Jews in Le Chabon, France. They were recognized by Yad Vashem as "Righteous Among the Nations" in 1984.

Simcha Unsdorfer was born in 1924 in Czechoslovakia. After his liberation from Buchenwald, he moved to England, where he became general secretary of Agudas Israel of Great Britain. His health was severely affected by his years in the camp, and he died in 1968 at age forty-four, survived by a wife and two children.

Rivka Wagner, born in 1924, was the daughter of a rabbi. When she was nineteen, she jumped from a moving cattle car to escape certain death in the concentration camps. She survived in Warsaw by pretending to be a non-Jew. She was reunited with her fiancé after the war, moved to Israel, and had four children.

Dr. Ruth Siegel Westheimer was born in 1928 in Germany. In 1939, at the age of eleven, she was sent to an orphanage in Switzerland, where she survived the war. Afterward, she moved to Israel and fought in the War of Independence. She later immigrated to the United States, where she became a well-known expert in sexuality.

Elie Wiesel was born in 1928 in Hungary and liberated from Buchenwald in 1945. From there he went to France and then to Israel, eventually settling in the United States. He was awarded the Nobel Peace Prize in 1986 for his activism in the cause of peace, atonement, and human dignity. He died in 2016.

Miriam Yahav was born in 1927 in Bialystok, Poland. She moved to Israel in 1949 and started a family.

Jakob Zim was born in 1920 in Sosnowiec, Poland. With his brother Nathan, he was sent on a death march to Buchenwald, where they were liberated. They immigrated to Israel in 1945, where Jacob fought in the War of Independence.

HERE ARE THE STORIES OF THE PEOPLE PICTURED ON PAGES 23-24:

Aron Goldman Bodner was a barber, born in Stary Sacz, Poland in 1906. He and his wife, Ruzi, were inmates in the Plaszow camp near Krakow before being deported to Auschwitz.

Joseph Broudo was born in Salonika, Greece. He was a merchant, married to Marie Varsano. The details of his death are unknown.

Mara Coblic, daughter of Yitzhak and Bracha Coblic, was born in 1936 in Chişinău, Romania (today Moldova). She and her mother died in the Chişinău Ghetto in 1940.

Helga Hamm was born in 1930 in Berlin to Willi and Margherita (Rubinfeld) Hamm. Helga was deported with her mother in 1942 and murdered.

Heinrich Jacoby was born in Belgard, Germany, in 1864. His wife **Margarete** was born in Eidtkonen, Germany, in 1875. They were deported from Germany and died in Terezin in 1943.

Hannah (Pilizer) Joskowitz was born in Łódź, Poland around 1900 and married to Yaacov Joskowitz. Their daughter, **Zhunia**, was born in the mid-1930s. Mother and daughter were both murdered in the Chełmno death camp.

Wiliam Wolf Zeev Kohn was born in Váncsod, Hungary in 1885. He was a merchant in Bratislava, Czechoslovakia, married to Maria Fisher. He was murdered in Auschwitz in 1944.

Florika Liebmann was born in 1934 in Szeged, Hungary, to Bela and Szerena Liebmann. She and her mother were deported and murdered in 1944.

Gabor Neuman was born in Békéscsaba, Hungary in 1940 to Alek and Margit Neuman. He was just four years old when he was deported to Auschwitz and murdered.

Bela Rodnianski was born in 1909 in Novhorod-Siverskyi, Ukraine, the daughter of Emanuel and Khaya. She was an accountant, living in Klintsy, Russia during the war. Bela was murdered there in 1941.

Artur Rubin was a trader, born in 1901 in Dobris, Czechoslovakia. His wife, **Truda,** was born in Dobris in 1907. They were deported to Auschwitz and murdered in 1944.

Zvi Segal was born in Romania and lived in Mihaileni. He was married to Nisla Nussem and made a living as a trader. He had one son who survived the Holocaust. Zvi was sent to Kopaygorod, Ukraine, and was murdered there at age seventy-six.

Boris Tzeitin was born in 1911 in Kharkov, Ukraine. He married **Maria Kogan**, who was born in 1915 in Senno, Belorussia. They lived in Nikopol, Ukraine. Maria was shot at Kamenka Dneprovskaya in 1941. Boris fell at the front in 1943 while serving as a technician in the Red Army.

Elly Weisz, the daughter of Iolanda Weisz, was born in Satu Mare, Romania. Elly was murdered in Auschwitz at age twenty-one.

Henryk Berush Szwarc was born in Zgierz, Poland in 1893. He was a clothing manufacturer in Łódź, married to Mala Eder. He was murdered at Majdanek in 1943.

LOST COMMUNITIES

HERE ARE THE STORIES OF THE COMMUNITIES LISTED ON PAGE 11:

1 **Warsaw, Poland:** The prewar population was 30% Jewish. Many Jews died in the ghetto, but the community managed to maintain a semblance of cultural life. When the deportations began, the Jews of Warsaw rose up and fought the Nazis.

2 **Sarajevo, Bosnia and Herzegovina:** This area was home to both Sephardi and Ashkenazi Jews, a prominent rabbinic dynasty, and a theological seminary. This vibrant community was almost entirely destroyed.

3 **Vienna, Austria:** Jews were prominent in all spheres of life and major contributors to its cultural and scientific achievements. Only a small Jewish community exists today.

4 **Chełm, Poland:** Chelm had a large Jewish community with a thriving Yiddish and Hebrew culture and a rich religious and political life, and was well-known in Jewish folklore. Today Chelm has no known Jewish residents.

5 **Salonika, Greece:** This two-thousand-year-old Jewish community served as a haven for Jews fleeing Spain during the Inquisition and was the most prolific Sephardic cultural and religious center in the world. This ancient, vibrant culture was completely destroyed.

6 Kielce, Poland: Jews in Kielce were involved in many industries and crafts. Most were murdered in the ghetto or in the camps. A postwar pogrom in 1946 in Kielce convinced many that Europe was still unsafe for Jews.

7 Riga, Latvia: Jews were well integrated into city and political life before the war. In 1941, 30,000 Jews were murdered in the forests outside of town, and all the synagogues were destroyed.

8 Wiesbaden, Germany: Wiesbaden was home to a small but flourishing Jewish community that played an active role in the city's economic, cultural, and sporting life. By June 1942, the city's entire Jewish population had been murdered or deported.

9 Kiev, Ukraine: Kiev was home to a thousand-year-old Jewish community. In 1941, more than 100,000 people were murdered at the ravine of Babi Yar near Kiev, including almost 34,000 Jews in just two days.

10 Prague, Czech Republic: Prague was home to Jews for more than a thousand years, in a community acclaimed for its literature. Today there is only a small Jewish community.

LEADER'S GUIDE

PLANNING AND PREPARATION

Timing: The ritual takes about 45 minutes.

Materials needed:
- Two candle holders: a fancy candlestick and an upside-down tin or glass cup or jar [pages 2–3]
- Rosemary sprigs [page 5]
- Wine [pages 5 and 21]
- Potato skins: peel the potato, rinse the skins, cook for one minute in the microwave [page 7]
- Salt water [page 7]
- Sweet tea [page 7]
- A child-made drawing that represents Judaism to them [pages 8 and 18]
- Unpeeled oranges: whole or cut into quarters or eighths. Bite-sized pieces are best for ease of eating. Tangerines work as well. [page 9]
- Fruits with pits: whole olives, dates, or cherries, not "pitted" (which have the pits removed). Bite-sized fruits are best. [page 13]
- *Yahrtzeit* candle [page 24]
- Bread: challah, or any good bread. This should represent the bread of our survival and community, not the bread of our affliction. [page 27]

On the table:
- Set out each of the items listed above.
- Set each place with separate cups for wine, sweet tea, and *(optional)* water for drinking.
- *Optional:* Pre-pour the wine and tea.

Tips:
- Reading aloud—whether by taking turns, reading together, or reading responsively—is a powerful way to engage participants with the material.
- In Help [page 15], encourage people to reach across the table to someone not sitting next to them.
- If desired, find additional pictures for *The Lost* in Memory [pages 23-24] at www.TeachTheShoah.org.
- In Memory [page 25]: Different communities follow different traditions regarding standing for the Kaddish. For this purpose, we are all mourners, and we stand for those who had no one to recite Kaddish for them.

OPTIONS FOR ADDED RICHNESS

The child's drawing as a family program:
Have a family program during the week
before Yom Hashoah where the children make
drawings of things that represent Judaism to
them. Choose one for the table, and hang the
rest on the walls.

Adding snacks or a meal: Recipes for
dumplings and cookies based on *In Memory's
Kitchen,* a cookbook from the Terezin Ghetto,
can be found at www.TeachTheShoah.org.

Adding movement: In Help [page 15], have
participants walk around the room and find
someone they don't know or don't know well,
to give them an opportunity to connect with
new people.

Yahrtzeit **candles:** Place a *yahrtzeit* candle on
each table. Be sure to put matches or a lighter
with each candle.

Bread: In Community [page 27], choose a
special bread to honor a particular community
–for instance, *tsoureki* (Greek sweet bread) or
babcia bread (Polish sweet bread).

Synagogue knocker: For the knocking in
Awakening [page 28], find a piece of wood
that resembles a shofar (but not a gavel) as a
schulklopfer would have used.

ALTERNATE EXPERIENCES

At home:
This ritual works as well in a home setting as
in a community context. For the best experience, follow it with dinner and discussion.

In a sanctuary:
- Have a few people lead and take turns
reading. Invite members of the congregation to read from the *bimah*. Multiple
voices add power to the story.
- Pass around as many of the symbols as are
feasible (e.g., rosemary sprigs).
- For symbols and experiences that cannot
be easily passed (e.g., spilling drops of
wine), perform them on the *bimah*. Invite
people from the congregation up for this
purpose.
- Give the child's drawing to someone in the
congregation to keep safe.

With another Yom Hashoah ceremony:
Pulling out and separately adding sections
of this ritual to another ceremony can add
richness to that commemoration. Some
suggestions to use:
- Light from Darkness *(especially the
mismatched candlesticks)* [pages 2–3]
- Resolve (*especially* Never Again)
[pages 16–17]
- Awakening [pages 28–29]
- Peace and Justice [pages 30–31]

For a younger audience:
A few minor changes can make the text age-
appropriate for a younger or less knowledge-
able group.
- Terror [pages 10–11]: Skip the initial
section and go straight to *The Lost Communities*.
- Awakening [page 29]: Cut the first stanza
from *An Affirmation for the Future*.

DISCUSSION GUIDE

ALSO SEE THE "CONSIDER" QUESTIONS FOUND THROUGH-OUT THE BOOK.

Light from Darkness: Why is it important to talk about how people lived as well as how they died? Survivor Pierre Sauvage said, "If we remember solely the horror of the Holocaust, we will pass on no perspective from which meaningfully to confront and learn from that horror." What did he mean by that? [page 2]

Origins: From where did this ancient hatred come? Discuss the deep roots of anti-semitism, how it was changing in the early twentieth century, and how it has changed since the Holocaust. [page 4]

Trouble: Notice that we have not mentioned individual perpetrators by name. Atrocities of this magnitude are only possible when many people consent and collaborate. Consider the many ways people collaborated with the perpetrators (e.g., *moving stolen furniture or taking homes after Jews had been forced out; sorting or selling goods sent back from the camps and killing pits; driving trains to the concentration camps*). Consider how small acts of willful ignorance and collaboration can slowly build to allow larger atrocities seem normal. How should this inform our response to seemingly isolated acts of bigotry today? [page 6]

Hiding: Thousands of children were sent by train, boat, or plane to apparent safety in countries across Europe and to the United States. The program to bring children into England was known as the *Kindertransport*. Parents were not permitted to follow. What are the ethics of rescuing children without their parents? [page 8]

Terror: Consider the options Jews had in attempting to escape the Nazis. Where could they go? How could they hide? Jumping from the trains, as Rivka Wagner did [see Stories, page 34], was a risky proposition. Most people who jumped were shot by snipers. Discuss the reasons that educated Jews and women had an easier time passing as non-Jews and how that limited the options of escape for many others. [page 10]

Strength: What does the existence of the ghetto library reveal about the people forced into such horrendous living situations? Discuss the idea of spiritual resistance: resisting the Nazis' attempts at dehumaniza-tion by maintaining religious, cultural, and educational practices. [See page 13, Yitzkhok Rudashevski.]

Help: Yad Vashem calls people who helped Jews and other victims of the Holocaust "the Righteous Among the Nations." Many, of course, will never be known, as many were unsuccessful in their attempts to help. Some paid with their lives. Yad Vashem's list of the known Righteous includes more than 25,000 people. [page 14]

Rescuers often risked not only their own lives but the lives of their loved ones. Consider a person's obligations to one's family and to people in need. When is it appropriate to put one's family at risk to help a friend or even a stranger? [page 14]

Resolve: Yad Vashem educator Lea Roshkovsky used to say that she could end the story of the Holocaust with the yellow star, because the yellow star made everything else inevitable. Once you allow people to be marked as "other," she said, they cease to be human in the eyes of the public and you can do anything you want to them. Discuss how separating people can lead to their dehumanization in the eyes of the rest of society and make bias-motivated violence more likely. [page 16]

Life: Consider the effect of this experience—the horror, the loss, the fear—on the survivors as they tried to move on with their lives. Many could move on; others, like Éva Heyman's mother, could not [see Stories, page 33]. Zsuzsanna Abonyi Ozsváth says she judges everyone she meets by whether she believes they would have saved her from the Germans. How do you think the Jews reconciled their hopes for the world with the world they discovered on liberation? [page 18]

Memory: Elie Wiesel said, "Do we know how to remember the victims, their solitude, their helplessness? They left us without a trace, and we are their trace." This is echoed in Jennifer Zunikoff's poem: "Only we can tell their stories now." What sort of obligation, if any, do we have to the victims of the Holocaust? [page 22]

Community: During the Holocaust, the Nazis divided community from community. Discuss the importance of solidarity between communities in nurturing humanity. [page 26]

Awakening: What does it mean to "be vocal torchbearers of love" and "to learn from evil to live for good?" How can we put these resolutions into practice in our own lives? [page 28]

Peace and Justice: Consider Rami Shapiro's injunction. How might this guide our choices in working for justice around the world? [page 31]

"During the first days after our return . . . we wanted at last to speak, to be heard . . . . Even so, it was impossible. No sooner would we begin to tell our story than we would be choking over it. And then, even to us, what we had to tell would start to seem unimaginable."
(**Robert Antelme**, Holocaust survivor, France)

ACKNOWLEDGMENTS

First and foremost, special appreciation goes to our third partner, Michael Fripp, for his insight, ideas, collaboration, and editing. This ritual would not be what it is without his help.

We would also like to thank Aviva Gutnick and the staff at Behrman House for believing in us and leading this project in an exciting direction. A special thank you to Jennifer Zunikoff for adding poetry to our wording. Thank you to our readers: Elaine Chernotsky, Mollie Marks, Ginny Redish, and Art Shostak. Thank you also to our testers: Rabbi Geoffrey Dennis, Don Dossey, Esther Fripp, Nathan Fripp, Rebecca Fripp, Debra Kaufman, Mollie Marks, Helena Shapp-Dossey, Gary Silansky, and Peta Silansky.

Thank you to Peta Silansky for unflagging support throughout this endeavor, as well as to Rabbi Geoffrey Dennis and the members of Congregation Kol Ami, who piloted this program.

This project was funded by an Incubator Incentive Grant from the Center for Jewish Education of the Jewish Federation of Greater Dallas and by the Teach the Shoah Foundation.

In addition, most sincere thanks go to the Yad Vashem International School of Holocaust Studies for teaching us an entirely new way of looking at the Holocaust. Special thanks to Lea Roshkovsky, Adi Rabinowitz-Bedein, Shulamit Imber, Ephraim Kaye, and the teachers at the International School for Holocaust Studies for inspiration and assistance.

ABOUT THE AUTHORS

Deborah Fripp is the president of Teach the Shoah and the Holocaust Programs Coordinator at Congregation Kol Ami in Flower Mound, Texas. Deborah has a BS from Stanford University and a PhD from M.I.T. in communication and learning in formal and informal settings. Her website, www.TeachTheShoah.org, provides resources on commemorating, teaching, and understanding the Holocaust for communities, families, and educators.

Violet Neff-Helms, known as Tante to the many religious school kindergarten children she taught for fourteen years, is a freelance writer and the executive vice-president of Teach the Shoah.

Both are alumna of Yad Vashem's How to Teach the Holocaust in Formal and Informal Jewish Education seminar.

SOURCES

2 Hannah Senesh: *Ashrei Hagafrur*, 1944.

4 Miriam Yahav: *My Daughter, Maybe You . . . A Young Girl in Auschwitz* (Beer Sheva, 1994), p. 5.

4, 9 Hannah Gofrit: *I Wanted to Fly Like a Butterfly*, by Naomi Morgenstern (Yad Vashem, 2011), pp. 5, 26.

6 Éva Heyman: *The Diary of Éva Heyman* (Yad Vashem, 1974), p. 80.

6 Yitzhok Rudashevski: *The Diary of the Vilna Ghetto* (Ghetto Fighters' House, Hakibbutz Hameuchad Publishing House, 1973), p. 19.

7, 13 The idea for both the potato skins and the fruits with an unbreakable inner core come from *Haggadah for the Seder for Yom HaShoah veHaGevurah*, ed. Jacobo Rubenstein, 2010.

8 Ruth Westheimer: *Roller-Coaster Grandma* (Apples & Honey Press, 2018), p. 15.

10 Sara Selver-Urbach: *Through the Window of My Home: Recollections from the Lodz Ghetto* (Yad Vashem, 1971), p. 122.

12 Rivka Wagner: Quoted to the authors by her daughter Malky Weisberg.

12 Simcha Unsdorfer: *The Yellow Star* (Thomas Yoseloff, 1961), p. 103.

13 Chaim Kaplan: *Megilat Yissurin–Yoman Getto Varsha* [Scroll of Agony–Warsaw Ghetto Diary], *September 1, 1939–August 4, 1942* (Yad Vashem, 1966), p. 202.

13 Yitzhok Rudashevski: *Salvaged Pages: Young Writers' Diaries of the Holocaust*, ed. Alexandra Zapruder (Yale University Press, 2015), pp. 217–18.

14, 20 Zsuzsanna Abonyi Ozsváth: From her talk at "Winning the War: America, Foreign Policy, and the Holocaust," University of Texas at Dallas, June 27, 2018.

14 Irena Sendler: Letter to the Polish Senate (2007), quoted in "Irena Sendler, Lifeline to Young Jews, Is Dead at 98," by Dennis Hevesi, *New York Times*, May 13, 2008.

14 André Trocmé: From the exhibits at Yad Vashem.

15 Elie Wiesel: From the foreword to *The Courage to Care*, by Carol Rittner and Sondra Myers (New York University Press, 1989).

17 The last blessing on the page comes from the Union for Reform Judaism's *Daily Blessings: For Social Action*.

22 Donia Rosen: *Forest, My Friend* (Yad Vashem, 1985), p. 94. The original reads, "Not a monument of marble or stone, but one of good deeds, for I believe with full and perfect faith that only such a monument can promise you and your children a better future."

24 Mary Elizabeth Frye: first printed in 1932 and subsequently adapted by various unknown sources.

26 Violet Neff-Helms: Excerpted from her unpublished poem "Dumplings," 2018.

27 Susan Cernyak-Spatz: In *Memory's Kitchen* (Jason Aronson, 1996), p. xxix.

28 Hanns Loewenbach: Quoted in his obituary, "Hanns H. Loewenbach," *Virginian-Pilot*, February 1, 2012. The original quote reads, "Evil does not need your help, just your indifference."

29 Elie Wiesel: From his Days of Remembrance Address, Washington, DC, 2001.

29 "An Affirmation for the Future": *Days of Remembrance: A Department of Defense Guide for Commemorative Observance* (Office of the Secretary of Defense, 1988), p. 20.

30 Martin Luther King Jr.: *Stride toward Freedom: The Montgomery Story* (Harper, 1958), p. 51.

31 Rami Shapiro: *Wisdom of the Jewish Sages: A Modern Reading of Pirkei Avot* (Harmony/Bell Tower, 1995), p. 41. An interpretive translation of a quote from Rabbi Tarfon from *Pirkei Avot* 2:16, referring to Micah 6:8.

31 The original quote from Deuteronomy 16:20 reads, "Justice, justice you shall pursue."

40 Pierre Sauvage: *Weapons of the Spirit* (Chambon Foundation, 1989).

41 Robert Antelme: *L'espèce humaine* (Gallimard, 1947), p. 3.

41 Elie Wiesel: From his Nobel Prize Lecture, December 11, 1986. The original reads, "Mankind must remember that peace is not God's gift to his creatures, it is our gift to each other."

CREDITS

Collection of the Yad Vashem Art Museum, Jerusalem, Photos © Yad Vashem Art Museum, Jerusalem: *View of Ostende with Boat,* 1935, by Felix Nussbaum (1904–1944), gouache on paper, 50x64 cm. Gift of Roger-David Katz and his wife Louba Moscicka, Brussels. *Camp Synagogue in Saint-Cyprien,* Brussels, 1941, by Felix Nussbaum (1904–1944), oil on plywood. Gift of Paul and Hilda Freund, Jerusalem. *Rear Entrance, Terezin Ghetto,* 1941-1944, by Bedřich Fritta (Fritz Taussig) (1906-1944), India ink and wash on paper, 51x36.5 cm. Gift of the Prague Committee for Documentation, courtesy of Ze'ev and Alisa Shek, Caesarea. *To the Man who Restored my Belief in Humanity,* 1945, by Yehuda Bacon (b. 1929), gouache, black chalk and pencil on paper, 22.1x30 cm. *Taleskoten,* 1944, gouache, charcoal and crayon on paper, 47.5x58.9 cm, and *Winter,* 1944, charcoal and crayon on paper, both by Zinovii Tolkatchev (1903-1977). Gifts of Sigmund A. Rolat, New York, in memory of his parents, Henryk and Mania, who perished in the Holocaust. *View of Buchenwald, a Few Days after Liberation,* 1945, by Jakob Zim (Cymberknopf) (b. 1920), watercolor on paper, 18.7x29.3 cm. Gift of the artist. *One Spring,* Gurs Camp, 1941, by Karl Robert Bodek (1905-1942) and Kurt Conard Löw (1914-1980), watercolor, India ink and pencil on paper, 14.4x10.3 cm. Gift of Annelies Haymann, Kiryat Bialik. *Liberation* and *Rose and Barbed Wire,* both by Shmuel Leitner. Reprinted with permission of Dr. Gabriel Leitner. Photos on pages 23-24 courtesy of Yad Vashem Photo Archive.

Shutterstock: background: ilolab; p2, 4, 14, 15: ESB Professional; p9, 27: Picsfive; pIV: Candles: chempina (candlestick), vectortatu (cup), Olli_may (candle), rosemary: aninata, cup: Bodor Tivadar, potato: cgterminal, tea: Stock-Nick, child art: vectorsicon.com, orange: Rina Oshi, cherry: Epine, olives: MoreVector, bread, challah: Olga_Zaripova; p1: Paul Crash; p6: Valik; p8, 20 (papers): LiliGraphie, p20 (city): vividvic; p26: Ungor; p31: Masterrr; p36: dikobraziy. Yahrtzeit: Ann D. Koffsky.

Cover art: Shutterstock, Jacob_09

"From Darkness into Light," by Chaim Stern, excerpt from "We pause in reverence" by Alvin Fine from *Gates of Repentance* © 1978, revised 1996 by Central Conference of American Rabbis. Used by permission of CCAR. All rights reserved. "From Tomorrow On," by Motele: *Through Our Eyes: Children Witness the Holocaust,* by Itzhak Tatelbaum, Yad Vashem, 2004, p. 89. Reprinted with permission. "They are gone," by Jennifer Zunikoff: excerpt modified from her poem "Leo Is Gone," written in loving memory of Leo Bretholz, March 9, 2014. "A Day Will Come," by Jennifer Zunikoff, 2018, Reprinted with permission.

A DAY WILL COME

a day will come
when the softest sounds
will be enough

when one lingering note,

a delicate dance
between two hands,

a leaf spinning in
the breeze

when one ringing bell

when one whispered poem
will be enough

to awaken each person
from that which is concealed

to bless this holy human
with wisdom that bursts

from the sacred well of justice

from the sweet, hearty, bubbling
subterranean spring that nourishes
the Tree of Life

(Jennifer Zunikoff)